A Season For Dreaming

A Season For Dreaming

Sermons for Advent, Christmas, and Epiphany based on the Second Lessons for Cycle A

Ken Lentz

CSS Publishing Company
Lima, Ohio

A SEASON FOR DREAMING

FIRST EDITION
Copyright © 2025 by
CSS Publishing Company, Inc.

Published by CSS Publishing Company, Inc., Lima, Ohio 45807. All rights re-served. No part of this publication may be reproduced in any manner what-soever without the prior permission of the publisher, except in the case of brief quotations embodied in critical articles and reviews. Inquiries should be addressed to: CSS Publishing Company, Inc., Permissions Department, 5450 N. Dixie Highway, Lima, Ohio 45807.

Library of Congress Cataloging-in-Publication Data
Names: Lentz, Ken author
Title: A season for dreaming : sermons for Advent, Christmas and Epiphany
    based on the second lessons for Cycle A / Ken Lentz.
Description: First edition. | Lima, Ohio : CSS Publishing Company, [2025]
Identifiers: LCCN 2025029390 (print) | LCCN 2025029391 (ebook) | ISBN
    9780788031298 paperback | ISBN 9780788031304 adobe pdf
Subjects: LCSH: Advent sermons | Christmas sermons | Epiphany
    season--Sermons | Common lectionary (1992). Year A | LCGFT: Sermons
Classification: LCC BV4254.5 .L46 2025 (print) | LCC BV4254.5 (ebook)
LC record available at https://lccn.loc.gov/2025029390
LC ebook record available at https://lccn.loc.gov/2025029391

For more information about CSS Publishing Company resources, vis-it our website at www.csspub.com, email us at csr@csspub.com, or call (800) 241-4056.

e-book:
ISBN-13: 978-0-7880-3130-4
ISBN-10: 0-7880-3130-9

ISBN-13: 978-0-7880-3129-8
ISBN-10: 0-7880-3129-5

*In memory of my sister, Sue Lowden, who
celebrated Christmas with gusto and joyful faith.*

Contents

Introduction

Luther once recounted a legend he heard about a "rude dunce" who once stood in church, and, unlike all those around him, did not take off his cap or bow down when the words of the creed, "et homo factus est" (and he was made man) were chanted. The devil himself stepped up to the man, hit him hard, and cursed him for his lack of respect and reverence upon hearing the great glad tidings, "God became man to save us from our sins." Luther's point was that even Satan could not fail to be amazed by so great a mystery. (WHAT LUTHER SAYS, Concordia Publishing House, St. Louis, Missouri, 1972, No. 4359)

Whether one displays amazement at Christmas Eve candlelight services, at the office Christmas party, or when tearing open wrapped gifts, we can all rejoice that millions will avoid the slap of the devil for standing around like a stick when the Christmas cycle rolls around on its yearly rounds.

The four Sundays of Advent invite us to prepare for the celebration, the twelve days of Christmas give us time to at least do something to express in word and/or deed that some folks in a little village near Bethlehem had a remarkable experience, and the Sundays of Epiphany invite us to tell the world about the miracle we call the "incarnation."

I hope that the following reflections on the season's epistles will inspire some to think about the age-old message of Christmas, a message which really is intended to point the way to our journeys to resurrection and a world foretold by a star and heavenly choruses.

Your fellow traveler on the way,
Ken Lentz

Tempus Fugit!

A preacher went up into the hills to bring the gospel to the mountain folk. He met an old mountaineer coming down the trail. "Are you a Christian?" Asked the preacher. "Heck, no... Christ. Christian lives up the road a piece." "No, I didn't mean that," replied the preacher, "I meant, are you lost?" "Oh, no," said the old fellow, "I've been here for nigh unto thirty years and I know every cow path like the palm of my hand." "Oh no," retorted the preacher, "I mean, are you ready for judgment day?" "When is it?" "Well, it could be today, or it could be tomorrow." The hill dweller pleaded, "please don't tell my wife. She'll want to go both days."

Timing is critical. This season of Advent directs our thoughts to the second coming of Jesus. Is he coming soon or will I have time to pay off the mortgage? Many before our era took the time to think about time. Virgil, for example, was a Roman poet who lived and died shortly before the birth of Jesus. He was born in 70 BC and died in 17 BC. His full name was Publius Vergilius Maro but we usually just call him "Virgil." He loved time, savored it, enjoyed it, and always wished for more of it. Raised on a farm, he took great delight in watching the shifting of the seasons. He wrote of the fields, the fresh wine just drawn from the jar, the water-brook running nosily with hoarse murmur, the violet blossoms mixed with saffron, and yellow garlands blended with crimson roses. He loved the rustic rhythm of the country and infrequently and unenthusiastically went for visits to the big city. He worked slowly on his poems, writing less than one line a day and felt the time slipping away from him. Therefore, he wrote, "...fugit irreparable tempus," or "time flies irretrievably." His time to savor the life he loved was fleeting. But he could at least hope for a "golden age" with cows chewing their cud and ripened wheat swaying in the breeze with a bright sun blessing undulating lanes winding between hill and dale.

Like our Amish brothers and sisters, Virgil savored the pacifism of country life, reverence for the gentle gods of rural life, and disdain for the urban and military life where "right and wrong are confounded." If he had read the words of the prophet Isaiah, he would have shared Isaiah's hope for the days when "they shall beat their swords into plowshares, and their spears into pruning hooks" (Isaiah 2:4).

Paul also believed that "time flies." "For salvation is nearer to us now than when we became believers; the night is far gone, the day is near"(Romans 13:11f.). One wonders if Paul, who was well versed in all things Greek, knew that Virgil the Greek poet had longed for a "golden age," and had envisioned the coming of a divine child who would be born to set all things right in the world. Paul's "golden age" was envisioned as the time when "salvation would come." Paul did not specifically encourage his readers to take up the tranquil life of agrarian morality but his exhortation to prepare for the day of salvation by living lives of honor without works of darkness, debauchery, and licentiousness might have sounded like the naivete of country folks.

In one of the "Peanuts" stories, Lucy started talking to Linus, listening with thumb in mouth and security blanket tucked against his ear. Lucy said, "I'm going over that hill over there and I'll find the answer to my dreams...someday I'm going over that hill and find happiness and fulfillment. For me, all the answers to life lie beyond those clouds and over the glassy slopes of that hill." Linus took his thumb out of his mouth, looked at the hill, reflected, and then said, "perhaps there's another little kid on the other side of that hill who is looking this way and thinks that all the answers of life lie on this side of the hill." Lucy looked at Linus for a bit and then turns toward the hill and shouted, "forget it, kid!"

Maybe Advent has no message for us. Perhaps there is just more of the same ahead. Maybe Isaiah, who saw the wolf dwelling with the lamb and a place where "they shall not hurt or destroy," (Isaiah 11:6,9) was on uppers. Maybe Virgil was unreasonably optimistic. Maybe Paul was disillusioned. But the hopeful blue of Advent dares us to believe that the resurrection of Christ is a foretaste of our "golden age."

Great thinkers have lamented the principle of "time flies." Andrew Marvell wrote of "time's winged chariot hurrying near." Virgil himself was afraid that he would not be able to finish his history of Rome before he died and, sure enough, he died on a trip to Greece at the age of 51. He had worked on his history for ten years without having completed it. Keats was haunted by fears that he would die before he had written all that he wanted to write and Robert Louis Stevenson wrote,

But now I pause a whiles in what I do
and count the bells, and tremble lest I hear
(my work untrimmed) the sunset gone too soon.

But the psychologists tell us that it is healthy to sense the rushing of time. Time is not supposed to lie heavy. It is healthy to keep right on moving. The healthy Christian will embrace the future without fear and joyfully anticipate the future. What we do about the present will shape the future. It seems to me that people who enjoy longevity are people who have always been busy in their lives. The best retirement is the busy retirement.

Once there was a Christian lady named Monica who stayed up all night and prayed in a seaside chapel that her pagan son would change his mind and not sail the next day from the northern coast of Africa for Italy. She feared that his departure for Italy would rule out his conversion to Christianity. But he sailed the next day in spite of her prayers. After a few years of study, he went one day to a garden and heard a child's voice tell him, "Take and read; take and read." He opened the writings of Paul to chapter 13 of Paul's letter to the Romans and vowed to abandon his hedonistic lifestyle. He went to Milan and introduced himself to Bishop Ambrose. He was taken by the bishop's kindness and returned to north Africa where later he was ordained as Bishop of Hippo. If Augustine had become a Christian later in his life, that would have been a great blessing, but we have greatly benefitted from his decision early in life to dedicate himself to the lordship of Christ.

A physician once visited an elderly man who was suffering from an attack of bronchitis. The doctor said that he would have to go to his office to prepare some medicine for the patient. The patient's wife asked, "Doctor, how soon can I come to get the medicine at your office?" "Well," replied the doctor, "Why don't you stop by in about a month for it?" "A month from now!" Cried out the wife in astonishment, "John could be dead in a month!" "Well, then, perhaps you could come in a week." "I beg your pardon," protested John from his bed, "but I might not live a week. Shouldn't I begin to take the medicine today?" "Begin today by all means," said the physician. "I only wanted to show you how false your own reasoning is, when you put off taking the medicine which the great physician has provided for you. For many years you have avoided a commitment for Christ thinking, perhaps, that you could make amends with God on your deathbed." "Besides this, you know what time it is, how it is now the moment for you to wake from sleep. For salvation is nearer to us now than when we became believers" (Romans 13:11).

The gospel of John seems to suggest that "salvation" or "the kingdom of heaven" is to be understood proleptically. "Time flies." Perhaps the kingdom of heaven is both: it is in the future, and it is in the moment when one grasps it. Virgil seems to have grasped his agrarian utopia before his untimely death. Paul certainly did. Paul wrote to the Romans and delivered in his own words. Not on a silver platter but upon papyrus, the words of eternal life. *Tempus fugit.* Time flies. We are invited to embrace the future now. We embrace "salvation" in the now and present when we proclaim it in word and deed.

Amen.

Foretaste Of The Feast To Come!

Betty had to leave Bob for a few weeks to go off to Minneapolis to take care of Uncle Harry, who was ailing. She asked Bob to promise to take care of the cat while she was gone. Bob promised. A week later Betty called to check in with Bob. "How's the cat?" she asked. "He died," answered Bob. "Oh Bob, how could you break the sad news in such a cruel way?" Betty replied. "How should I have done it?" asked Bob. "Well, you could have told me that the cat was upon the roof and that you couldn't get him down. Then you could have told me the next day that you got him down but that he broke his leg in the process but that you took him to the vet and the vet said that he would be all right. And the next day you could have told me that the cat took a turn for the worse and passed quietly and peaceably away." "Oh," said Bob. Then Bob asked, "by the way, how's Uncle Harry?" "He's up on the roof and we can't get him down."

In Matthew 3 (1-12) we read about the crowds who gathered at the Jordan and eagerly confessed their sins and thereby received assurance of God's forgiveness washed upon them by the waters of the rivers. But the Pharisees and Sadducees were denied entry to God's grace. For some, the washing in the river would not be a "foretaste of the feast to come," a liturgical promise used in some Christian churches.

But Paul emphasized future hope, not John's "wrath." Like Betty's suggestion to use more gentle language, Paul, writing to the believers in Rome, speaks about the hope anticipating the coming of the "root of Jews but for Gentiles as well" (Romans 15: 12).

The meals (Acts 2-46-47) shared with one another by the early believers were meals that marked their harmony bound by hope (although the Corinthian Christians practiced a degree of exclusion according to 1 Corinthians 11). We Americans envision our thanksgiving feasts to be feasts of familial harmony, even though the celebration of peace in the family is sometimes not what it should be.

For me, two feasts come to mind. The worst meal I ever had was served on a trip to the Soviet Union in the fall of 1989, right before the wall came down. Our transfer from Moscow to Uzbekistan from the Moscow airport occurred late at night. After several hours of waiting, my tour group was finally ushered onto the plane where we all had to scramble to find unbroken seats. Our red-eye special flight featured greasy cold chicken and water served in plastic cups. Our arrival in Samarkand allowed two hours of sleep time in our hotel before breakfast. Most of us were troubled by diarrhea. Sensing our unhappiness, Tanya our Siberian guide promised a gala meal that evening. Expectations ran high. We began to envision something more exciting than plain cooked tough meat, grainy bread, boiled potatoes, and overcooked runny vegetables. Our spirits soared. We sat at table that evening and watched as the usual plain cooked tough meat, grainy bread, runny vegetables, and boiled potatoes appeared before us. The "gala" treats turned out to be unlimited caviar and vodka. More "gala" dinners were promised, all featuring only the usual fair garnished by more caviar and vodka. But we rejoiced with Tanya, who savored the vodka and had to be extracted by us from her bed mornings. We speculated that our tour was for Tanya a respite from Siberia's bears and log cabins.

The best meal I enjoyed was served at Chanson's restaurant in west Hollywood in 1993 in the intimate company of Ronald and Nancy Reagan, Jimmy Stewart, Ricardo Montalban, and about 100 other guests. The dinner was hosted by Bob and Delores Hope who hoped to raise a considerable amount of dollars to support the renovation of the Vatican library in Rome. The guests were treated to spectacular table bouquets (not consumed by the guests), course after course of delectable perfectly prepared and served meats, vegetables, cheeses, and parfaits accompanied by the finest wines. Notwithstanding the religious purpose of the dinner, the meal would be my best nomination for "a foretaste of the feast to come" award.

But Paul's feast surpassed Hollywood's best efforts. Paul's feast was a feast of hope. This season of Advent has traditionally been decked out in the color of purple, the color of confession of sin and appeals for mercy from God. The present trend is to feature the color blue, the color of the sky whence our Savior will come again. Blue is the color of hope. But it is difficult to transition from purple to blue. Even Martin Luther, who championed hope, struggled constantly from his *"anfectung,"* his obsession with despair. The story was told about one of his attacks of melancholy which he endured sequestered in his study. His wife, Katharina, suddenly appeared at the door shrouded in black. Luther turned, startled, from his desk, "Woman, who is dead?" She replied, "God is dead." The great reformer laid down his pen. "Why do you speak of God being dead?" Katie retorted, "You have been acting that way as though all hope were gone, and God was dead."

We all sometimes struggle with doubt and few believers walk around with a glow of hope radiating from them like a sun corona. Luther and Mother Teresa experienced days of doubt and melancholy. There's an old story about two duck hunters who once got into a boat to head down the Santee river in South Carolina for a place called tranquility. They left home about 1 am one winter night and planned to travel ten miles on the ebb tide in order to reach their destination around daybreak. When they left, the stars were out but soon they were lost behind a dense fog. But they felt safe as long as they were going with the tide. But after a few hours, a fog crept in and they could no longer see the shoreline. Big waves began to rock the boat. Attempts to reach shore failed. The boat was shipping water by the gallon. But the boater said to his guest, "Never mind, Cap'n, it will be daybreak soon."

Certainly, the new believers in Rome were not manic. They didn't float around all day in bliss. They sometimes quarreled with one another. Jewish converts were not sure that Gentile converts were kosher. Paul quoted four passages from the Jewish scriptures that pointed to Gentile inclusion. The Roman converts struggled in their attempts to figure out how to live new lives in the light of the gospel. They already sensed persecution in the air (Romans 12:14). They squabbled about clean and unclean food (Romans 14). Life was not a bed of roses.

But they sensed the feast to come. Sir Walter Scott was a sickly youngster who believed that he would never amount to much. One day, Robert Burns came to visit at his house and read a little poem that Scott had written. Burn's eyes began to lighten up and he lay his hand on the young man's head and exclaimed, "Ah, my boy, I'm sure you'll be a great man in Scotland someday." That word of hope set Scott on the road to greatness.

Paul's feast is a feast of unity. "May …God…grant you to live in harmony with one another…so that together you may with one voice glorify the God and father of our Lord Jesus Christ" (15:5f). I once led a group on a tour of south Germany. When our group arrived in Oberammergau for the night, the only Catholic participant suddenly died of a heart attack in his room after dinner. A physician pronounced him deceased. I summoned the local priest who administered last rites. I prayed with his wife and daughter.

Some in our group called me aside and insisted that I instruct his wife and daughter to accompany his remains back to California. The mood in the group was depression. A friend had died. The trip would continue under a gray cloud of loss. I took the group the next morning to Sunday services in the Protestant church. The pastor prayed for the deceased and his family. After services, some in the group mentioned that the church bells had called Henry home. Others were happy that Henry had experienced Germany, his lifelong wish (but he missed the last four days of the tour.) The group, consisting mainly of parishioners of my congregation, turned their attention to his wife and daughter who, having permitted Henry's transit to Munich for cremation, remained on the tour. The tour group, in the middle of an unexpected turn of events, translated their bewilderment into a support group for Henry's family. The experience became a great manifestation of harmony. It was a foretaste of the feast to come. What will be the feast to come? It will be the realization of hope, the realization of harmony, the realization of glory and peace. We gather as believers in our various settings around the Lord's table. We receive the bread and the wine: one bread and one cup. There is hope. There is harmony.

Amen.

Advent 3

James 5: 7-10

Second Coming: Patiently Waiting

Our text from the letter of James started with an admonition: "Be patient, therefore, beloved, until the coming of the Lord" (5:7). James underscored a widespread anticipation that Jesus was coming again the second time soon! A minister once preached enthusiastically about the second coming: "Thunder will boom. Lightning will strike! Rivers will overflow! Flames will shoot down from the heavens! There will be storms, floods, earthquakes!" A little girl sitting next to her mother in the front pew looked up and asked, "Mommy, do you think we'll get let out of school?" One wonders how a lot of children would respond if they were told, "Santa's not coming this year, Johnny; Jesus is coming instead." "Shucks!"

There are a lot of unknowns and speculation about the identity of James. Was he the brother of Jesus or perhaps a cousin — Jerome? Was he an apostle or a first-century teacher in the church? Was he even a Christian? (he only referenced "Jesus" twice and wrote a letter about Jewish morality.) His Greek was beautiful...too classic to be the second language of a Jew. But the greatest consensus is that James was, in fact, the brother of Jesus, the James who presided over the council of Christians in Jerusalem, the one whom Paul met after Paul's conversion on the road to Damascus, and the one to whom Paul took his collection for the Gentile Christians (Acts 21). Barclay seemed to lean in the direction that favored the "letter" as a sermon "pressing the moral duty" of believers (see William Barclay, *The Letters Of James And Peter*, Philadelphia: The Westminster Press, 1960, pp. 3-33)

For James, Jesus was the one who was coming soon on the clouds of glory. His listeners (and readers) seem not to have feared lightning, flames, and earthquakes but were eager to meet their Messiah.

Therefore, James urged patience. The patience of a farmer (v. 7). I experienced firsthand the patience of farmers in the first parish to which I was called in 1970 in northwest Ohio. Even the landscape seemed patient: it stretched out in all directions, vast fields of mostly soybeans meeting the horizon with only a few clumps of trees breaking the monotony. The farmers seemed patient. They watched the rains come and patiently waited until they came again. One morning I awoke in my huge white-framed parsonage to noise outside my window. Farmer Casper was in my driveway patiently waiting for a ground hog to exit from beneath my car. His dog Frosty was barking at the ground hog while suffering frequent sharp claws jabbing at his nose. Casper suggested that I stand behind him until he got a clear shot in case the bullet should ricochet against the garage cement floor. Casper was cool and collected; he was patient. Finally, bloodied Frosty flushed the beast out and it was dispatched easily to ground hog heaven.

On Sunday afternoons, I joined the Caspers in their car in order to take an exhilarating cruise on country roads and take note of their neighbors' soybean growth. The slow-speaking, cool and calm mentality of the farm folk was a pleasure to behold. Their patience was a blessing. My great ideas for changes in the parish were met with soft-spoken, kindly, responses. When without checking with the church council first, I hired a new organist from a small college about seven miles away for a weekly compensation of $20, the council took my brash behavior in stride and agreed to somehow find the extra money.

James urged the patience of the prophets. Were the prophets really patient? Nathan didn't hold back when he confronted the adultery and murder of David. James specifically points out the patience of job in whom God manifested his purpose (v. 11). Normally, Job, strictly speaking, did not conform to a popular understanding of "patience." A re-reading of his story depicts Job as one who verbalized frustration about his lot in life. Calamity after calamity, Job just wished that God would let him alone (Job 7:17-19). He begged God to stop tormenting him (Job 19:1). He resented what had come over him, he rejected the thought offered by his friends that he had somehow offended God, and he could not understand why God would desert him. But in the end, he repented and his riches were returned to him and more. Job as a model of patience must be understood as patience "which can breast the tides of doubt, sorrow, and disaster and come out with faith still stronger on the other side" (Barclay, *The Letters Of James And Peter*, p. 125). Verse 11 indicated that James' understanding of patience included endurance. "Indeed, we call blessed those who showed endurance."

I was serving a congregation in Castro Valley, California, when the great earthquake of October 17, 1989, violently shook the bay area. I missed the excitement because I was on a street returning to the church from an errand in hayward. I noted that traffic lights were swaying back and forth but, otherwise, saw and felt nothing. I complained to my co-pastor about the outage of some of the lights and he responded, "Where were you? We just had an earthquake!" The Nimitz freeway in Oakland was rendered impassible when sections of the upper deck collapsed directly on the lower deck, a section of the bay bridge fell into the bay, and the marina district went up in flames; 63 lives were lost. A few weeks later, I met a lady who bitterly complained about all the calamities in her life. First there was the earthquake and then a crane fell in downtown San Francisco. "Oh no," she cried out, "now what's next? I'm just going to go into my house and not come out anymore." I wondered why she was so upset. She was untouched by the earthquake and a crane did not fall on her house.

The kind of "patience" advocated by James is the patience that gets us up and going again when the going gets rough. It is the patience of faith that strengthens us when the chips are down. It seems to me that the readers of James' letter were encouraged by him to embrace the ups and downs of life. Perhaps it is in those moments that patience fills us with endurance and the will to bravely face the future. It is the patience that we experience when we are fully engaged in life. We do not sense its full power if we stand on the sidelines.

I've never been able to get excited about football games. Why? Because I don't know the members of the teams. I never met them. I've never seen them in any of my congregations and they're just a bunch of numbers on a field of battle fighting a war that, for me, is slow and boring. But I once witnessed a game so exciting that I ripped off the buttons of the coat on the guy standing next to me. It was one of the last games of the season when I attended Capital University. It was the game against our arch-enemy, Otterbein, a little EUB college just a few miles down the creek from our campus. Those Otterbein guys were really bad and evil. They used to come to our campus in the middle of the night and toilet paper the whole place. But our guys were great; they were the good guys! I knew all of them. Most of them were in one or more of my classes (the campus only accommodated 1,600 students.) And I knew that our guys could lick the tar out of our adversaries! What a game! Otterbein was ahead. And then we were ahead. They regained the field. Then it was the fourth quarter! We surged ahead in the last few minutes of the game, and we won! We knew we would. We only had to "endure" until the bitter end!

That's what the prophets did. They endured until the end. James didn't mention Jesus by name but certainly he could have. Not only did Jesus accomplish his mission on earth but he will come again to give sight to the blind, give mobility to the lame, clean the lepers, give hearing to the deaf, and release the poor from their bondage. Advent is the time to be "patient," to commit to endurance, to anticipate the second coming. The farmer patiently waits for the crops to ripen; the prophet patiently awaits fulfillment. And so do we.

Amen.

Getting Ready For Christmas

The buck private at the military requisitions' office answered the phone. The voice said, "Hello, we need twelve vehicles in the parade square immediately. Two of them must be limousines." The private retorted, "what do you need the limos for? To haul those fat-slob generals around in, I bet." The voice on the other end of the line responded, "Soldier, do you know who this is speaking?" "No, I don't." "This is General Wilson." The private then asked, "Do you know who this is speaking, sir?" The general answered, "No, I don't." The private replied, "See you 'round, fatso," and hung up.

The line of authority is important. In his greeting to the believers in Rome, Paul established his authority. He made it clear that he was a fellow believer but he also made it clear that he had the upper hand on the inside story about Jesus. Paul had been "set aside" as apostle, especially chosen by Christ to be a teacher and leader in the church. Paul was on his way to Rome and he wanted the Roman "saints" to be prepared to be taught by a credentialed pedagogue, but not dull or pedantic.

Christmas faith begins with trust. Our Old Testament lesson for Advent 4 reminds us that Paul trusted the messages of the prophets, most certainly the prophecy of Isaiah. One of the kings of Judah, Ahaz, did not trust the authority of God. Instead of turning to God for help in his confrontation with the empire of Syria, he decided to form an alliance with Assyria. Isaiah, the prophet, confronted him and challenged his faith. "Why did you decide to trust earthly assistance instead of trusting God? Let me give you a sign that God is more trustworthy than the

Assyrians." "Oh, no, that's all right Isaiah, I just don't want to bother God right now." Isaiah responded and said, "I'm going to give you a sign anyway: a maiden in Judah will give birth to a son and his name shall be called Immanuel, 'God with us.'"

Paul knew the point of the story: God will send himself, "Immanuel," "God with us." Paul knew the Jewish scriptures forward and backward. He trusted the prophecies of the prophets and those prophecies foretold the coming of Jesus, the one of human lineage and the one of divine nature. Paul trusted what he believed to be promises "good as gold" because they were promises from the highest "authority," heaven itself.

A Baptist deacon once advertised a cow for sale. The potential buyer was a Presbyterian elder who asked, "How much do you want for the cow and how much milk does she give?" The Baptist responded, "I want $150 and she gives four gallons a day." "Fine, I'll take the cow home and bring back $150." "But," asked the Baptist, "how do I know you'll bring back the money?" "Oh, you can trust me; I'm a Presbyterian elder." The deal was struck and the Baptist went home and asked his wife, "What is a Presbyterian elder?" She answered, "Oh, it's about the same as a Baptist deacon." "Oh, no!" Exclaimed the Baptist, "I've lost my cow."

Actually, there's no reason to not trust Baptist deacons and Presbyterian elders and Paul reminded us that there is no reason not to trust the prophecies of the prophets.

Christmas faith is grounded in action. The apostle Paul grounded his life in the obedience of faith and his faith led to action. The experts believe that Paul was in Corinth in about 55 AD and would reach Rome no later than 61 AD. The facts are unclear about the realization of his plan to go on to Spain. But no one could possibly exceed the dedication of a first century traveler bound and determined to endure the hardships and risks of travel in order to deliver the gospel in person. He traversed dangerous valleys, along thief-infested roads and over sometimes turbulent seas in primitive vessels. Only a faith accompanied by action could get the job done. Paul may not have known the details of Jesus' birth as recorded later by Matthew and Luke in the late 70s, but he knew that the Messiah had come, an incarnation at birth, not an adoption at Jesus' baptism. And although of the lineage of David, the Messiah experienced a humble birth and life, but yet a "king" greater than David, revealed in his resurrection.

In 2022, protesters in Iran were being quickly condemned to death by Iranian kangaroo courts because they dared to protest injustice at the hands of the government. In 2024, protesters in Israel demanded greater efforts by their government to gain the freedom of hostages kidnapped on October 7, 2023, and protesters around the world demanded the end of the horrific slaughter of innocent Gaza strip residents by the IDF. The passion of believers in Christmas should be greater than the elaborate efforts to make one's Christmas tree or home the best on the block. The preparations to receive Jesus as the baby born in the straw of a cattle stall in Bethlehem should include the passion of prayer and the passion of witness to an event which changed the world. It is a story that includes human elements juxtapositioned against the glory of angels singing in the heavens. Paul's witness included both.

Christmas faith is courageous faith. If Paul had known the story of Joseph, he would have admired the faith of Joseph. Joseph and Mary weathered the three stages of a normal Jewish marriage. They may have been promised to each other at an early age by their parents. They may have even not known each other. Then, at some point, they ratified the arrangement without exercising the right of rejecting the plan. At that point, the engagement was binding but had to last a year. Only a formal divorce could dissolve it. Mary and Joseph were still in the engagement stage when Mary became pregnant. Courageously, Joseph continued the "marriage" because he learned of God's involvement. Like Paul, Joseph was willing to weather the storm of ridicule, rejection, and slander. Joseph's faith was courageous faith.

A woman once visited a zoo and was indignant and out-raged when she saw the monkeys playing with dice in their cage. She complained to the zookeeper that the monkeys were gambling. The zookeeper defended the policy of the zoo man-agement by explaining that the monkeys were only "playing for peanuts."

We are called not to "play for peanuts." The Christmas event is more than fun and games. It is an event that compels serious faith. It is about acknowledging the sovereignty of God, taking action to advocate on behalf of the poor, stepping up when others are exploited, and showing courage in the face of threats and intimidation, spoken or unspoken. It is faith that enthusiastically accompanies the placement of the Bethlehem creche. It is faith for every day of the year. I knew a parishioner some years ago who kept her house decorated all year round because she did not want to forget her Christmas faith. "What child is this, laid to rest on Mary's lap?" It is the child in whom we have trust, who inspires us to action, and in whom we cou-rageously believe all year long.

Amen.

Christmas And The Godly Life

There was once a monk named Antonio from Modena. Someone gave him two beautiful mountain donkeys which he used at Advent time to gather baskets of goods from the rich to give to the poor. On Christmas Eve, he decorated his two donkeys and gathered dozens of children to light the way through the dark streets. He carried a staff from which hung many tiny bells. Summoned to their windows and doors by the tinkling of the bells, the locals gazed with eyes full of tears upon the parade of donkeys, candles, and children. The impoverished inhabitants received their gifts with thanksgiving and blessed Antonio as he made his way from door to door. Antonio continued his Christmas mission every year until his death, a mission celebrated to this day in Modena with presents carved from wood or made from plaster.

Perhaps Antonio was inspired by the words from Paul's letter to Titus, in which Paul named Christ's incarnation as the launching pad for Christian morality. "For the grace of God has appeared…training us to renounce impiety and worldly passion" (Titus 2: 11f). Paul didn't reference the story about Mary, Joseph, and the baby. Jesus, for him, was "the grace of God (which) has appeared." Therefore, the Titus text is a Christmas text. Titus was a Greek disciple of Paul who Paul left behind in Crete to organize and lead communities of believers. He had accompanied Paul on the mission trail, gathered collections for the poor of Jerusalem (2 Corinthians 8: 6, 10), delivered a letter from Paul to the Corinthians (2 Corinthians 8:16) and went with Paul once to Jerusalem to meet church leaders (Galatians 2:1).

For Paul, Christmas was the "appearance of God's grace," a designation more in line with the gospel of John – a more poetic and lofty proclamation of Jesus' origins in John 1 than the beloved story we tell every year with the creche under the tree or before our churches' altars. Paul's almost parenthetical reference to the "appearance of God's grace" supported a theory that John's beautiful poem was based upon an earlier expression about the origin of Jesus than the birth narratives which first appeared in the accounts of Luke and Matthew in the 70s. Paul theoretically wrote his letter to Titus while in prison in Rome in 60/61 AD.

The letter to Titus embraced Christmas that was about "incarnation" instead of about the birth story which began, "in those days a decree went out from Emperor Augustus..." (Luke 2:1). Luther said, "He (Jesus) descends to the level of our nature and becomes a member of the human race! It is an honor which no angel in heaven shares" (*What Luther Says*, Vol. II, Concordia Publishing House, Saint Louis, Missouri, 1972, 2758).

If the believer preferred to focus upon the "light" of Christmas rather than displaying the Pascal manager scene, this text is made for him/her. Once there was a rich farmer in Germany who heeded God's call to be a missionary. After serving poor German immigrants in Paris, France, he accepted a call to become the shepherd of a small congregation along the Ruhr river. Rebounding from the loss of all four of his children within a week in 1869, he agreed to become the director of a small home for epileptics. Before his death in 1910, the small endeavor became a vast complex of buildings housing epileptics and the hopelessly mentally and physically handicapped known as Bethel-Bielefield, the model for homes of mercy all over the world. Friedrich von Bedelschwingh the elder once penned these words:

> *Das is das wunder der heiligen nacht,*
> *Dass in der dunkelheit der erde die helle sonne scheint.*

"The miracle of Christmas Eve is that the bright sun shines in the darkness of the earth." Bodelschwingh's legacy pointed to the second point made by Paul in his Titus letter:

> Christmas encourages a response. Because "the grace of God has appeared, bringing salvation to all," believers will "renounce impiety and worldly passions ...and live lives that are self-controlled, upright, and Godly"(2:12).

I couldn't afford to go to college after high school graduation and was lucky to get a job working for a large paper-producing corporation in Dayton, Ohio. I actually saved enough money in one year to pay for my first year at college. The girls in the office pool were excited for weeks anticipating the office Christmas party. In those days, my life centered around activities at the small-town high school and the youth activities at church. Christmas was celebrated with prayer, religious devotions, and simple gift exchanges at both church and high school. The party at church included an exchange of small gifts, Christmas sugar cookies, and non-alcoholic punch. The office Christmas party omitted Christmas carols, prayers, and scripture readings, but offered plenty of hard liquor and much smooching, interesting posterior pinching, and holiday sexual inuendoes without regard for marital pairing. Santa Claus made no appearance. I guessed that nobody had ever read about "impiety and worldly passions." The party was a foretaste of future Christmas to come in a culture which no longer necessarily references either the birth in Bethlehem or the incarnation, the appearance of God's grace.

I once met a woman at a reception. She was raised in Vienna, Austria. On Christmas Eve, 1946, she and her family were gathered in their cold apartment in front of a tree which her mother had chopped down in the woods. For one evening, they made an effort to forget their plight or the plights of many trapped in post-war Europe. It was Christmas. They sang

Christmas carols. And after they had gone through a round or two of the old favorites, they feasted on pudding made from cornstarch without sugar and they drank tea without the benefit of sweetener. And yet they were happy. They sang — and sang and sang. They had a roof over their heads; many did not. They had each other; many had lost family members in the war. And most important, they had the Christ child in their hearts; many in that city of rubble and ruins had hearts too frozen with loss, despair, and poverty to offer a place for the Christ child. And, although their dad was missing, they were so happy and they kept right on singing and singing, warmed by each other under the feather beds.

Certainly, that family was poised to rebuild their lives that would be "self-controlled, upright, and godly."

Many of us are not lucky enough to experience the hardship and challenges that bring us to the brink of losing everything. Titus must have certainly preached Paul's gospel to those in Crete who had their own rubble and ruins to contend with. Titus had a message to share. Paul, his mentor, urged him to preach a message about the appearance of God's grace. Certainly, the vision of something so pure could inspire lives free from the chains of impiety, worldly passions, and ungodliness.

Paul reminded Titus that the response to the appearance of grace was bridged between the incarnation of Jesus at one earthly moment and the future "manifestation of the glory of our great God and Savior, Jesus Christ" (v. 13). The incarnation was a sign of that which would be. The godly life of a believer would therefore be a signpost to the future. The godly life of the Christian is itself an "incarnation" of the way things would be. To live an ungodly life would be a denial of the future. The godly life is how we get ready to slide into the next "manifestation of the glory" to come. To stand in the presence of someone's godly life is to already have one foot in the life and future to come. One can look at Christmas both ways: one can see the lighted plywood manger scene in the front yard of someone's house and say, "now, that is Christmas!" Or one can look at the bright lights on the Christmas tree and say, "now, that is the brightness of God's grace!" Scripture offers us two ways to get the message. And that is God's gift to us.

Amen.

Jesus, Still Lead On

The jet airliner raced through the sky. Suddenly a puzzled look appeared on the pilot's face. The co-pilot asked, "What's the matter?" The pilot answered, "I don't have any idea where we are or where we are going! Do you?" "As a matter of fact, no, but we're sure making good time getting there."

Some people have no idea where they are going, but they are making good time getting there. People are funny. They don't plan ahead but they want the front of the bus, the back of the church, and the middle of the road. Luther's theology was dualistic. The humanist side of him recognized human potential and worth, but the scriptures compelled him to recognize the human inclination to do the wrong thing. "Sin…is like a man's beard, which, though shaved off today…yet grows again…as long as a man lives, such growth of the hair and the beard does not stop. But when the shovel beats the ground on his grave, it stops. Just so original sin remains in us and bestirs itself as long as we live, but we must resist it and always cut off its hair" (*What Luther Thinks*, Concordia, St. Louis, 1972, Vol. III, 4176).

Our text today from Hebrews offers hope for the beard that does not go away. Basically, little is known about the author of Hebrews except that the writer was fully immersed in both greek and Jewish culture, wrote to presumably the Jewish converts in Rome about 80 BC, and seemed to be a scholar writing to scholars. (Most experts do not believe that the writer was Paul.) Those addressed in this seem to be caught between two persecutions, possibly between the reign of Nero (64 AD) and the crackdown of Domitian (ca. 85 AD).

But the author knew a lot about Jesus. Three strong themes pop from the pages of the letter: Jesus was a high priest (after the order of Melchizedek), Jesus was acclaimed as one who was exalted (not resurrected), and Jesus was the "pioneer" of our salvation (2:10 and 12:2). A lot of preachers and theologians have waxed eloquently about the priesthood of Jesus and about his exaltation, but it seems to me that our text tells us something about ourselves.

His role as "pioneer" *(archegos)* put him right in front of us on our human journey. Will Durant once said that Jesus was like the steeple of a little white church in the valley below the hill where he used to spend his summers. His daily walk down the path toward the village guided by the white steeple symbolized his human yearning for the goal and purpose of life. People are different from the rest of the animal world because people can direct their appeals to a power for hope and strength.

Jesus could be the steeple that can guide us even in the midst of our separation from God. Jesus led us back. Jesus was the one who could deal with sin, the beard that doesn't stop growing. Jesus' identity was tied to our identity. He was a child of God, and we are children of God. God sanctified him and God sanctifies us. He was a brother to us who are his brothers and sisters. He didn't appear to come to the aid of angels, but he appeared to come to our aid. One might conclude that Jesus became like us in order to reveal what we have the potential to become. He became like us in order to model true humanity.

He demonstrated the conquest of temptation. "Because he himself was tested by what he suffered, he was able to help those who are being tested" (v. 18) Shortly after I received my driver's license, I ran through a traffic light. It was one of those "questionable" situations. Was the light still yellow or was it red? I gave into temptation. I ran the light. I was caught. I obeyed the blinking lights and pulled over. The police officer did not share my conviction that the light was still yellow. Before my court date, I was advised by a friend that I should plead "no contest." Surely the judge would recognize my inno-cence. I pleaded "no contest." "Fine," said the judge, "go pay the court clerk $50."

I once heard the story about a young applicant for a pro-motion in a bank. He was under consideration for a position left vacant by a retiree. He arrived early for the interview and went to the cafeteria to have lunch. One of the bank officers observed him taking a piece of butter and hiding it under his meat to avoid the surcharge of a few cents. He gave into temp-tation and lost his job and the promotion. The temptation to run an "orange" light. The temptation to hide butter under the meat. Small stuff.

Our text addresses the bigger temptations. The temptation to cheat on one's spouse. The temptation to cheat at tax time. The temptation to lie one's way through a difficult situation. The temptation to proclaim oneself "good" when one knows that I, among others, have fallen short of the glory of God.

Jesus, the one who was the "pioneer," the one who ven-tured ahead of us, and led us to freedom. It was "freedom from sin, death, and the devil," as the reformation leaders would put it. Jesus was the high priest in order "to make a sacrifice of atonement for the sins of the people." Freedom from sin is a relative thing. We know that we can never be free from sin. We can, however, forge ahead, trusting the "pioneer" to absolve us of our sins. He went ahead of us to plead for us before the father. And we know that his pleas are heard.

Our earthly "chains" are a metaphor for the sin that holds us fast. I went with a church group behind the iron curtain in 1970. I met theology students in Erfurt. I met a member of the faculty at the University of Wittenberg. I stole away from my group in Leipzig and took a night commuter train secretly to meet with Johannes Hempel, at that time the director of the preaching seminar. All of those I met told me what it was like practicing their faith in the German Democratic Republic. One student in Erfurt told me that he was about to refuse conscription in the army. The faculty member and his wife in

Wittenberg told me about Stasi spies everywhere, while they served me sugarless cake. Dr. Hempel showed me photographs he had taken secretly of the destruction of a Gothic church to make way for a new library. I heard the stories of rights denied from those trying to witness to their faith in a secular culture. They couldn't express themselves freely. Dr. Hempel's son was not allowed to go to university because he was confirmed in the church. Believers couldn't get the jobs they wanted. They weren't even supposed to go to church. Where was freedom?

They lived in the shadows and darkness of a communist secular anti-religious state, but they were free. They were free to love God and to know his love for them. I was in California when the wall came down in late 1989 and I wept for joy for those I had met behind the Iron Curtain. We who now live in a democratic land can nevertheless be bound to cultural mores that compromise the values taught by Jesus. The struggle to live in the light of freedom would be a lost battle where it not for the "pioneer" who leads the way.

Jesus showed us the way beyond death. "Since therefore, the children share flesh and blood, he himself likewise shared the same things...(in order to)...free those who all their lives were held in slavery by the fear of death" (v.14f). I once heard about an eighteen-year-old boy who drowned while experimenting with an aqualung. He was a mild-tempered, gifted lad full of great promise. When his father looked down upon his body that afternoon, he cried out in anguish, "Why did this have to happen? Why have you been taken away from us when you had so much to live for?" A young minister arrived upon the scene and tried to comfort the distraught father by placing an understanding hand upon his shoulder and saying, "It is God's will. You must understand, it is God's will." The father, with face distorted from grief and anger, raised his eyes to the sky and shouted, "God, if you could do this, if you could take my only son from me, then I want nothing to do with you, ever!"

I have heard those kinds of words many times in my ministry. I don't think it is "God's will" that anyone die. But death is inevitable. Things have gone wrong in the world. The story of Adam and Eve in the garden and the story of Noah and the ark remind us that we have chosen universally to go our separate ways. But the pioneer can pull us to the side of our misguided path and lead us in another direction. Death will have to be faced. He endured death. But in his "exaltation," (or "resurrection," if you prefer) advanced beyond death. He invited us to follow him through that dark valley. The father who lost his son could (eventually) release his son into the hands of Jesus who led the boy through the dark waters and up and out of the darkness into the light of life. The father who lost his son had to impute his own trust in God prematurely to his son.

William Barclay wrote that Christ was the "pioneer" who was the one, according to the Greek word, that started a city so that others may live in it, who started a school so that others may study in it, who went before the army to clear the way, or who is the sailor who jumps into the water with a line to tie the ship (*The Letter To The Hebrews*, Westminster Press, Philadelphia, 1957, p. 26). Jesus was the pioneer; he showed us that temptation can be overcome, that freedom is actual, and that death is not the victor.

Amen.

Christmas Backstory

A little boy took some Christmas cookies from the cookie jar without permission. His mother caught him. She asked him, "Son, don't you know God saw you take those cookies?" "Yes," replied the youngster, "but he didn't see me eat them. I ate them under the table."

God sees our misdeeds; even at Christmas he doesn't give us slack. Experts in child rearing tell us that eye contact is important when communicating. "Johnny," says the parent when insisting that the child stop playing, "look directly at my eyes. It is now 7:30 pm in twenty minutes, you will stop playing, put aside your toys, and go directly to your bedroom to go to sleep." Eye contact is important when instructing the child but also when announcing happy news. Paul established eye contact with God in his message to the Ephesians.

The mystery of Christmas, the mystery surrounding the rustic birth of a child in a backwater town in Palestine, the mystery of the nativity so beautifully, majestically, and poetically presented in John's hymn of incarnation at the beginning of his gospel, brings us to our knees in awe. The mystery of Christmas is announced in Pauline words at the beginning of his letter to the Ephesians. He told the backstory of Christmas.

God had a plan. Christmas has its origins in the shadowy times long "before the foundation of the world" (v.4). The focal point of the plan was Jesus, who appeared on planet earth as God revealed in human language.

An army chaplain arrived home suddenly after many months overseas during World War 2. He called his wife to announce his arrival during the night before Christmas. A plan was made to surprise the kids. When the children gathered around the tree on Christmas morning, they noticed a big lump in the white sheet upon which their presents were resting. The lump began to grow and from the pile of presents emerged their long-absent father. Their memories and images of their father became wishes come true. There stood their daddy.

The hopes and dreams of the inhabitants of the world was made manifest in Jesus, the one sent as planned "before the foundation of the world." During a thunderstorm the belltower of a church in Harmony, Minnesota, was struck by lightning, setting off the automatic chimes. Paul's disclosure about the "mystery of (God's) will" revealed the greatness of God. The birth of Jesus was no second thought. It was not a plan, according to Paul (or perhaps a disciple of his) quickly conceived. It was "a plan for the fullness of time, to gather up all things in him, things in heaven and things on earth."

This lofty portrayal of God is beautifully imagined in paint upon plaster, the Christ Pantocrator, prominently looking down upon the faithful in eastern orthodox churches. The babe in the manger concealed in the form of an infant is the one who majestically brought God's plan into fruition. Christ is the benevolent God who, through the suffering of his son, would reveal God's mercy and forgiveness. "In him we have redemption through his blood, the forgiveness of our trespasses, according to the riches of his grace that he lavished on us." Only a God portrayed in glory could bestow universal mercy upon the world. The daddy who emerged from under the sheets beneath the tree appeared to bestow love and protection upon his children. Lofty was the plan and lofty is Christ.

God chose us. Some scholars think that Paul's letter to the Ephesians was originally a letter by one of his disciples to the church in Laodicea, or perhaps to all the churches in Asia. When it landed in Ephesus, the receivers attached their church to the greeting. But, nevertheless, the letter reflects the thought of Paul also to be found in the letter to the Colossians. The writer introduced a metaphor to help explain the relationship of believers to Christ. "He destined us for adoption as his children through Jesus Christ."

The concept of "adoption" struck a chord in his listeners. The metaphor is also used in the letter to the Romans (Romans 8:15). Adoption was a widespread practice in the Roman and Greek world. The Roman process was strictly and legally proscribed. The adoptive father had to apply for the right to adopt in a complicated legal ceremony and then had to go to a magistrate to present his case. If the right was granted, the adopted son lost the rights of his previous family, became the heir of his new father, and was regarded as having no life before his adoption. He was "owned" completely by his new father. In the case, likewise, of the new convert to the Christian faith, the old life is gone and there is only the new life dedicated to the will and authority of God (*William Barclay, The Letter To The Romans*, Westminster Press, Philadelphia, p. 105f).

This "adoption" reveals our identification with God. Rabbi Abraham Heschel taught that God wills his connection to humans to be evident. "You cannot worship God and at the same time look at man as if he were a horse." (*Moral Grandeur And Spiritual Audacity*, Farrar, Straus, and Giroux, New York, 1999, p. xvii). Heschel even suggested that God needs us, his "divine pathos." His daughter claimed that was the central theme of his theology (ibid, p. xxii). In order for God to be God, then God must be bound to us. Our bond to him might be metaphorically referred to as "adoption."

I once heard the story of a girl in an orphanage. Once a month the children were dressed up and presented to visiting potential couples thinking of adoption. The girl became concerned by the time she was eight or nine because she was never chosen for adoption. She did her best to look attractive; she wore a clean and starched dress, washed her hair, pursed her lips, and rubbed color into her face. Luckily, she was finally spotted and taken on as a trial. She was overcome with joy and hope. Finally, she had a real home with a real mother and a real father! A few weeks later, she came skipping home from school one afternoon and spotted her little suitcase, packed and sitting on the stoop of the house. She was returned to the orphanage. Years later, she recounted her story to a circle of friends. There was not a dry eye. But she spoke up, "I was returned several times to the orphanage but then I learned that there was one parent who adopted me and would never reject me. He was Jesus. I have learned that his commitment to me is everlasting, and I have never felt abandoned."

We are chosen to praise him. Paul wrote, "...so that we ... might live for the praise of his glory" (v. 12). If we accept the theory that Ephesians is a circular letter, Paul spoke as a Jew writing to not only the Ephesian Gentile converts but to all those newly committed to Christ in many places. The one who commends his or her life to Christ will "live for the praise of his glory."

Those committed to Christ will receive blessings from "the heavenly places" (v. 3). Once a hopeless alcoholic went to a New York physician seeking a cure. The doctor referred him to a hospital, sobered him up, and administered psychotherapy. But when the physician released him, he admonished his patient, "I've done what I can do for you, and I think you're better. But there's about five percent of your personality that I can't get at. And judging from my experience, that five percent will trip you up sooner or later."

The young man pleaded, "Isn't there anyone who can help me, anyone at all?" The doctor smiled. "There is a doctor," he said, "but he's very expensive. He'll take all you have. I think you know the one I mean." The man left the hospital and walked through the city streets until darkness fell. It was a cold, rainy, miserable winter's night and he wanted a drink desperately. He stopped at a church and approached the door. He was conflicted. He wanted to enter but he did not want to enter. In desperation, he wrote upon one of his business cards, "Dear Dr. Jesus, please help me." He dropped the card through the letter-slot and burst into tears. An indescribable feeling of warmth, relief, and release came with the tears. A spiritual blessing from the heavenly places? His desire for a drink never came back.

I once knew a faithful parishioner who died at the age of 99. The church was packed at her funeral. For eight years I had been personally strengthened by her words, her love, and her testimony when I visited for home communion. She wouldn't let anyone get away with a compliment. She insisted that she was a sinner and when she sometimes "slipped up" and said a word that she thought was critical or could even remotely be interrupted as critical, she apologized profusely. If it ever occurred to her that she had offended someone, she would get on the phone or write a note of apology. She had come to California as a young girl from a village in Denmark to be someone's nanny. She married a fellow Dane and raised three boys. By the time she died, her husband and two of her sons had preceded her in death. She accepted her lot in life in faith and shared her faith through compassion. When I visited her at her small apartment, she put on the coffee and brought out the tin of cookies and we sat together at a small table to read the devotions for the day. No wonder she was honored by all of us as "Grandma Damkier."

Christmas is really about the Grandma Damkier's of this world. I am sure that there were at least a few of them in every church that read the letters of Paul. What was God's plan? He planned from the beginning to bring joy to those in the world who would live to praise him. Not that God is fickle. The one who praises him is the one who brings hope, joy, and happiness to the world.

Amen.

The Road To Baptism

Some American Presbyterian pastors attended a seminar in Scotland. One afternoon, a group of them left the lecture building to explore their surroundings on foot. They came to a stream spanned by a temporary bridge. Failing to note the notice warning about the poor condition of the structure, they began to cross it. A groundskeeper ran toward them and shouted, "Stop! Get off the bridge!" One of the ministers replied, "It's all right. We're allowed to be here. We're Presbyterians!" The caretaker answered, "I'm no' caring aboot that, but if ye dinna get off the bridge, you'll all be Baptists!"

The story introduces a discussion about baptism. What is the bridge to baptism? The account of the baptism of Jesus in our Matthew text (3:13-17) presents today's topic. The Acts account (10: 34-43) suggests a road to our understanding of Christian baptism.

The road to understanding baptism began with the spotlight with Jesus. Peter's missionary journeys took him to Joppa where he took up lodging from a certain tanner named Simon who lived by the seaside. Peter went up on Simon's roof to pray. He fell asleep while waiting for his lunch and God revealed to him a vision of four-footed animals, reptiles, and birds all snuggled peaceably together in a sheet. While contemplating the meaning of the vision, Simon called up to Peter to tell him that some men sent by a centurion named Cornelius stationed at Caesarea had come for a visit. The visitors explained to Peter that their boss wanted the apostle to come and offer some religious clarification. At Caesarea, Peter renounced Cornelius' high opinion of him and then explained that even though it was unlawful for a Jew to hang out with Gentiles, he came anyway. It was an *aha!* moment for Peter who suddenly understood the meaning of his rooftop vision.

Peter quickly put together an overview of the importance of Jesus. After all, he was confronted by a crowd of Roman family members and friends of the centurion. It was a teaching moment. Peter explained that out of love, God sent Jesus to preach and to heal. Jesus was crucified but rose from the dead. Peter witnessed the resurrection. The life, death, and resurrection of Jesus is a sign that God forgives sins and that a new relationship between sinners and God has been revealed.

Peter's message focused on the person and meaning of Jesus. Segundo Galileo, a Chilean priest has put it this way:

> ...*it is only through Jesus of Nazareth that we can know God, his words, his ideals, his demands. It is in Jesus that the true God reveals himself; all-powerful but at the same time poor and suffering for love; absolute, but also someone with his own human history, someone close to every person.* (*Evangelical Catechism*, Augsburg Publishing House: Minneapolis, 1982, p. 157).

A man was backpacking through the mountains alone and continued his trek at nightfall. In the darkness, he became lost in a rainstorm. He fell and lost his flashlight. He fell to the ground and groped for the object on his hands and knees. While he crawled on wet earth, a flood of lightning illuminated the mountainside, and he saw that he was inches away from a cliff. The next lightning flash revealed the destination of his hike that day, a cabin only a few hundred yards away.

The road to understanding baptism begins with the spotlight on Jesus, whose task it was to reveal forgiveness of sins and bring humankind out of darkness into the light.

The road to baptism continues with a vision of light. Those gathered at the house of Cornelius were moved by Peter's impromptu sermon. Peter's Jewish companions were shocked to hear that God loved Gentiles as much as he loved Jews. The Gentiles, suddenly filled with enthusiasm by the Holy Spirit, asked to be baptized.

The account of the multiple baptisms at the house in Caesarea says a lot about baptism. The account of the event implies that everyone was baptized, even children who were likely there. Those who advocate the practice of infant baptism will point to this account and also to the account of the conversion of Lydia at Philippi. "She and her household were baptized"(Acts 16:15). And Paul's jailor's "entire family were baptized"(Acts 16:33). Backed by the practice of the early leaders of the church, it appears to me that both infant and believers' baptism are valid.

I once wanted to encourage a friend of mine who had become active in a non-denomination church in a big city. The church was not affiliated with the mainline church in which he was raised but I was happy to see him connected to a congregation. I even accompanied him and his two young sons to worship every Sunday evening for a few months. He, as a single parent, enjoyed the company of other single parents, who, as a group, attended a single-parent Sunday school class, worshiped together at services, and ate together at simple meals served in the fellowship hall. I joined the group at worship and ate with them after services.

At one such meal, with all singles gathered around a round table, we were joined by a single mother who I had not yet met. Her curiosity seemed to be aroused when I was introduced as a pastor in a mainline church. She asked all members of the group to relate when they had been saved. I suspected that she had embarked upon some kind of a plan. Each person at the table related the day and time in their lives when they had been "saved." Finally, it was my turn. I explained that I was saved when I was baptized. "When were you baptized?" "I was baptized as an infant," I confessed. My inquisitor displayed an expression of extreme shock. Several uncomfortable sounds were released. The other folks at the table suddenly were interested in shoes or other objects on the floor.

I recognized a teaching moment. I presented baptism as an event entailing two actions, metaphorically like a horse and a buggy. I suggested that all mainline churches teach that baptism involves the consent of the believer. In infant baptism, the buggy comes before the horse. The sacred administering of water takes place in the context of the faith of those who present the baby. Some churches even believe, sacramentally, that the Holy Spirit plants the seed of faith in the baby. However, the horse must be attached to the buggy. The infant baptized must affirm (or, confirm) his or her baptism at a moment or *kairos* moments in life. However, in the case of believer's baptism, the faith would come first and then, the baptized person, when "repenting" (come to trust in a merciful God), and affirming that repentance by going into the water, continues the lifelong baptismal process (suggested by the day of Pentecost, Acts 2) and by our text for the day.

At any rate, Cornelius and his folk came to bask in the merciful love and forgiveness of God, the forgiveness of God announced by the baptized Jesus.

The road to baptism continues with us.

Three members of the clergy were "discussing" the issue of abortion. The Catholic priest insisted, "I believe life begins with conception." The Methodist said, "I believe that life begins when there is a discernible heartbeat and when other vital organs seem to begin functioning." The other Protestant (denomination not disclosed) concluded, "Life begins when the kids leave home, and the dog dies."

Our texts suggest that life begins with baptism. It certainly did with Cornelius. A nervous new preacher spoke from the pulpit upon which was a pitcher and glass. As he preached, he kept on gulping until the pitcher was empty. An elderly parishioner remarked to friends at the end of the service, "The sermon was good, but it's the first windmill I ever saw that was run by water."

When baptized, we become those whose lives are powered by water, the water of baptism.

Baptism emphasizes our personhood. Sometimes people and institutions dehumanize us by treating us only as objects, as means of production, or as numbers. We are more than these. We are people who have a relationship with God. In baptism, God calls us by name and we become known to him.

Baptism makes it clear that our worth depends on God's promises, not on our views of ourselves or the views others have of us. (*Ecumenical Catechism*, p. 242)

God wants to make us whole. Baptism brings rebirth. There are those who make a distinction between "water baptism" and the "baptism of the spirit." No matter. Christians may differ on how much water it takes, or whether one is baptized before ability to confess faith or after one comes to faith, but all agree that baptism is an integral component in the life of faith.

The celebration of the baptism of Jesus is a celebration of the appearance of the one at the edge of the Jordan who came to bring us also to the Jordan, to the living water. There may be other ways to begin the Christian life of service, of proclaiming the coming of the kingdom in word and deed, but it seems to me that baptism is a good starting point. And it all began that day when two cousins met at the water's edge.

Amen.

Enriched In All Things

A pastor once met an inactive church member at the supermarket. He tried to be gentle as he asked, "I haven't seen you in church for quite a while, John. Is everything all right?" "Well, pastor," said John, "I've decided not to go to church anymore because there are so many hypocrites there." "Oh, don't let that keep you away," replied the pastor, smiling blandly. "There's always room for one more, you know."

Paul might have been smiling blandly as he made his opening points to the believers in Corinth. He had already been in Corinth for eighteen months (Acts 18) in about 50-51 AD. He was writing from Ephesus about four years later, having heard about some problems in the community. With tongue in cheek, he commends the new community that is "enriched in (Christ)" (v. 5) and "not lacking in any spiritual gift,"(v. 7). Yes, of course, the converts were enriched in Christ and were not lacking in any spiritual gift but those blessings seemed to be, at the moment, on the back shelf. Paul's letter revealed that he had learned that they were split into angry factions (1 Corinthians 11: 18f) , perhaps morally in conflict with the gross immorality of the Vegas lifestyle (1 Corinthians 5:9), had turned worship into party time, (1 Corinthians 10:7), were arguing about whose gifts were greater than others (1 Corinthians 12-13), and were even suing each other (1 Corinthians 6: 1-8) they seem to be somewhat too attached to the local paganism and given to a tendency to bicker with one another.

But Paul began his letter on an optimistic note. He seemed to say, "Before I get down to the down and gritty of your scandalous behavior, let me remind you that in Christ you have been sanctified and dedicated to Christ, and called to be saints."

"Called to be saints"(v. 2). Not yet saints, perhaps, but on the way to be saints. Meant to be saints. It sounds like Luther's *"simul justus et peccator"* teaching.

Christians are divided into two parts: an inner being, which is faith, and an outer being, which is the flesh. ... but since faith exists in our fleshly nature and we still live on earth, we at times feel evil inclinations, such as impatience and fear of death. ... therefore Saint Peter says here: you are entirely pure and have a complete righteousness. Therefore, contend henceforth with your evil lusts. So, Christ., too, says in the gospel of John (13:10): whoever is washed must also wash his feet. That the head and the hands are clean is not enough (*What Luther Says*, Concordia Publishing House: Saint Louis, 1972, Vol I, 702).

Evidently the Corinthian believers were between washing their hands and their feet. But the dilemma faces us all. We are just like the Corinthians. We are "sanctified", but we are also sinners. That is the mystery of the Christian life.

We are imperfect. One foot is on earth and one foot is in heaven. The problems of the Corinthians are realities in church life today. In one of my congregations, there was a great dispute initiated by the new carpet in the church "parlor." Some members insisted that cookies should no longer be served in the refurbished room, lest cookie crumbs be ground by foot into the new floor covering. Others felt that the new room had been updated so that its ambience could be enjoyed. I took a stand and became the leader of the "cookie party." My party won but I'm sure there were some who grumbled every Sunday, watching on the sidelines with terror, in abject fear that the new carpet would be tarnished.

But, certainly, there are greater conflicts. I heard about a pastor who was dismissed because of accusations of plagiarism in his sermons. During the great charismatic conflicts of the late '60s and early '70s, some congregations were split right down the middle. I only know about one congregation which remained healthy because its members wisely decided to agree to disagree. One of my own cousins stood up in his congregation and shouted at the pastor, claiming that he was not saved because he did not have the gift of speaking in tongues. The pastor took an early retirement. Five families left the congregation and joined another non-mainline congregation.

It's best to be honest about these realities. A newcomer to the neighborhood decided to look for a church home. He made his fourth visit. Just as he sat down in the last pew of his visit, the congregation recited together,"Lord, have mercy upon us for we have sinned and have left undone those things which we ought to have done." The visitor sighed a sigh of relief and said to himself, "Thanks be to God. I've found my crowd at last."

Paul appealed to the Corinthians to admit their faults and try harder to conform to the life in Christ, but he would surely have felt that he was making progress if he found out that the "sinners" in Corinth had at least admitted their wrongdoings.

Christ is perfect. Paul's appeal is to the perfection of Christ. Christians confess the perfection of Christ in the words of the Nicene creed.

> We believe in one lord, Jesus Christ.
> the only son of God,
> eternally begotten of the father,
> God from God, light from light
> true God from true God,
> begotten, not made,
> of one being with the Father;
> through him all things were made.
> (*Evangelical Lutheran Worship*, Augsburg
> Fortress, 2006, p. 104).

The Nicene creed sums up what Christians believe about the person of Christ, but there are other ways to confess his nature. There was once a tiger cub, left to fend for himself when his mother was killed by poachers. He was adopted by a herd of goats. He thought that he, too, was a goat. He munched grass with the goats, butted heads with the younger goats for recreation, and even bleated in a strange sort of way. But his inner voice said, "something isn't right here; this isn't the kind of life you are supposed to be leading." But he ignored his inner voice and thought it to be pure fantasy. Then one day another tiger appeared at the edge of the clearing. It was a mature tiger who had no self-image problems. The mature tiger knew he was a tiger and he was supposed to chase goats to get his dinner. He roared the earth-shaking roar of his species, bounded out, and scattered the goats into all directions. But the tiger cub stayed put; he didn't run for cover. The roar from the edge of the forest had stirred a lost memory in his soul. In that moment was born the possibility of becoming a real tiger. He wanted to grasp the new and greater life challenging him from the clearing's edge. Christ is the one who calls us to live life with him. The perfection of his life can be made manifest in us.

In union with Christ, we can be enriched in him. Paul challenged the Corinthian believers with the model of life presented by Christ. They could put aside their differences; they could live in harmony. They could ignore the sacred prostitutes with torches who descended every evening down from the temple of Aphrodite dominating the cityscape. They could stop enriching the pockets of lawyers and save money by prayerfully beginning the process of Christian reconciliation. Even though they were a band of immature believers, they could enter the land of sainthood.

A man caught in a western town for sheep stealing was punished and branded with the letters, S T, "sheep thief," upon his forehead. He was scorned by the townspeople and embarrassed when strangers asked the meaning of the letters. He made a conscientious effort to live a Christlike life. Through the years he built a reputation for integrity and trust. One day a stranger came to town and asked the townsperson the meaning of the "S T" stamped upon the head of the man who had just passed on the street. The local guy scratched his head and said, "I don't really remember too well; it happened so long ago. I think the letters are an abbreviation of the word, "saint."

There are some New Testament scholars who think that Paul somewhere along the line met Titus who told him that all had become well in Corinth because chapters 1-9 of 2 Corinthians suggested that some kind of reconciliation had been worked out. No matter. The message to us is clear: the line between saint and sinner can be crossed. Once a hunter lost in a forest sat down in desperation at the edge of a raging river. He looked longingly at the pelts he had collected and, in despair, felt that all his efforts were no longer of any use. He could never sell his pelts. He was hopelessly lost. His life was over.

Suddenly an old woman stood at his side. Her skin was the color and texture of an unpolished boot. She pleaded, "Put me on your back and carry me across the river. If you do, you will no longer be lost." The hunter looked at the raging river and replied, "No, I cannot risk it." The woman began to cough and fell to the ground and begged to be carried across. "No," he insisted. Her cough and twisting became alarming. She asked again. The hunter thought, "this old granny must have suffered a lot in her day," and he relented. "Crawl on my back, but remember that if your bones fall apart in the water, there will be no way of retrieving them." He entered the swirling waters. The weight upon his back was like a lifeless corpse already in the coffin. He could barely place one foot ahead of the other. Amazingly, each step was easier. The weight upon his back became ever more bearable. When he reached the other side of the river, the figure upon his back slipped off and had become a beautiful young maiden. The hunter had crossed to a better life. His pelts and his gun were still on the opposite shore, earthly burdens best left behind.

Christ called the Corinthians to discard their petty disagreements, distance themselves from the world of distraction around them, and celebrate the new life of sharing, laughing, and praying together at their meals of love. Blameless in the eyes of God, they were free to celebrate together until the day of our lord Jesus Christ. Their life together could serve them well until that day when they would be "enriched in all things."

Amen.

The Unfractured Church

There were once two neighbors who had been feuding for more than twenty years. One day a revivalist came to town and one of the two antagonists was persuaded to go and was converted. The next day he appeared at his neighbor's house with two cows and a horse. "I have come to repay you for one of your cows which wandered into my pasture more than twenty years ago. I am sorry that I kept that cow, and I have repented of my sins and I want to make things right." The other neighbor was truly surprised and said, "You old thief! I will certainly take the cow in payment for the one you stole but why the extra cow and the horse?" "They are yours," said the first neighbor, "as interest for the cow I stole. The Bible says that we should repay double for what we steal and that is why I have brought you two cows. I brought the horse hoping you will use it to ride down to the tent revival. If you are converted, maybe you will return double all the chickens and pigs you have stolen from me through the years."

Hopefully, the attempt for reconciliation by the converted neighbor restored peace to the fractured relationship. What are the hopes for reconciliation between fractions of the universal church in our own day? Recently, the issues surrounding same-sex relationships have caused fracturing in the US in the Episcopal, the Lutheran, and the Methodist communities. Old bones of contention about the ordination of women, the interpretation of scriptures, and the nature of authority in the church still divide contemporary churches.

Fractures in the church are not new. The apostle Paul in the middle of the first century must have scratched his head when he, for example, heard about dissention in the new Corinthian community of believers.

Paul insisted that the church have one leader. He was visiting in Ephesus when he heard about contention in Corinth from some snitchers, friends of Chloe. The church seemed to be at odds about leadership. There were four groups. According to commentator William Barclay, those who claimed Paul as their leader and inspiration were probably newly converted Gentiles. That makes sense because Paul's cardinal proclamation was the inclusion of the Gentiles in the kingdom of God.

The second party were those who had been fascinated with the allegorical teachings of an intellectual Jewish teacher, Apollos, from Alexandria, who heard about the new apostolic teachings of the "way" from Priscilla and Aquila in Ephesus. Barclay suggested that these were intellectual Jews who were fascinated with Apollo's clever interpretive mastery and application of the Jewish scriptures. At this early point in the spread of the Christian message, students of teachers like Apollo began to frame the new faith into a philosophical and doctrinal system (Barclay, *The Letters To The Corinthians*, Westminster: Philadelphia, 1975, p. 14f).

The third party were those who claimed Cephas (Peter) as their leader and were likely Jews who found Peter's teachings more in conformity with their desire to stick to the observance of Jewish law. The "Christ" party, identified by Paul, may simply be Paul's way of saying, "If you want to declare yourselves followers of a particular leader, then name Christ as your leader, the one to whom you belong"(ibid p. 15). Naturally, that Paulist point is the point raised by all true ecumenists today who advocate a sense of unity be professed by all Christians. Why should Christians today bicker and fuss about who is right? Just accept all those who profess Christ as those in the one, universal church.

Paul taught that all eyes should be focused on Christ. If all proclaim Christ as leader, then all are on the same page and, therefore, have subscribed to one purpose, one mission, one focus. That focus is Christ. Once a pastor went to see a man who had been excommunicated from the church because of alcoholism, an old Norwegian who had suffered a massive stroke. He had lost his speech and was confined to bed in the home of his daughter. When the pastor offered to read from scripture, the man raised from his pillow, made a terrible guttural sound and knocked the New Testament out of the pastor's hand. The minister did not give up. He made a second visit the next day. Same response. The pastor toyed with the thought that perhaps the old duffer might respond positively to something that brought home to him the faith of his youth. On attempt number three, the pastor brought his wife. The two of them prayed before entering the house. In the stroke victim's room, the offer to read from the Bible was again dramatically rebutted.

With a nod from her husband, the wife began to sing an old Norwegian hymn. The bedridden man turned his eyes to the woman at the foot of the bed. He listened. Tears began to gather in his eyes. He fell back on his pillows and began to weep like a child. Prayers were allowed. The scriptures were read. Other visits followed. The man died trusting in the grace and mercy of God. The eyes of the man had been encouraged to focus on Christ.

Once a young man made a commitment to follow Christ while worshiping in his little village church. On the day following, he approached a classmate named Sandy Jones, a red-haired, awkward fellow, and asked Sandy to accept Christ as his Savior. Sandy responded, "Well, I don't know, John. Perhaps I will." The next day Sandy appeared in the little church and made a commitment to Christ. He walked across the floor of the meeting house and took John's hand and said, "I thank you, John. I thank you, John."

John left his town and became a biblical scholar and seminary president. He always returned to his town and the place of his boyhood in the summer. He made it a point to greet Sandy, the big awkward, red-haired farmer who repeated, "Howdy, John, I will never forget you, John." When John later in years lay on his deathbed and was asked about his life, he said, "I think the sound sweetest to my ears in heaven will be the welcome of Sandy Jones as he will thrust out his great hand and say, "Howdy, John. Thank you, John. I thank you, John.""

Several biblical commentators on this text have pointed out parenthetically that there it seems that the contenders for leadership in Corinth did not argue among themselves. Paul, Apollos, and Cephas (Peter, probably on his way to Rome) taught with one accord: the eyes of the faithful were to be always on Christ, the cornerstone of the church.

In Christ is embodied all truth. On October 31, 1999, the Lutherans and the Catholics formally announced and celebrated in Augsburg, Germany, the document, the joint declaration on the doctrine of justification. Paragraph 15 reads,

> ...together we confess: by grace alone, in faith in Christ's saving work and not because of any merit on our part, we are accepted by God and receive the Holy Spirit, who renews our hearts while equipping and calling us to good works.

Surely similar declarations in all corners of the universal church, in song, in prayer, in sermons, and in ecumenical statements, have pointed to Christ as the center of faith, the embodiment of all truth.

Christ is the great mediator. Once a pastor was troubled because of two rival factions on his church council. One side always opposed whatever position taken by the other side. The pastor prayed about the problem. At the next council meeting, when some very important issues were on the agenda to be discussed, he went to the meeting early and placed a large picture of Christ at the front of the room. When the meeting started, he said, "Tonight I want all of you to remember that you are here not for yourselves but to work for the cause of Christ. On each matter coming to a vote tonight, I want you not to look at one another but at Christ and ask yourselves how Christ would want to you to vote on that motion." Each time, when a vote was about to be taken, the pastor turned and looked at the picture of Christ and the eyes of the council members followed his gaze. For the first time in months, the members of the two rival factions abandoned their partisan loyalties and voted in the light of their professed loyalty to Christ.

Once a Catholic bishop was invited to speak at a protestant youth rally. He asked everyone in the hall to imagine a wheel with spokes. He then noted that the spokes of the wheel come together at the hub of the wheel. Likewise, the closer the various expressions of the universal church get to the hub, which is Christ, the greater will be the realization that there is one church, one baptism, one Lord.

The church in Corinth and the church today can be the unfractured church if all eyes are on Christ.

Amen.

Rags To Riches

A millionaire was once asked how he got rich. "Well," he said, "I began by buying peanuts for 25 cents a bag and selling them for one dollar. I worked long hours and all holidays. However, it took me five long years to become a millionaire. "You mean, it took that long to build up your peanut sales business?" Asked the interviewer. "Not really," replied the businessman, "my father died and left me a chain of hotels."

Many of us dream about getting the big break. We wish, "when my ship comes in..." or "when an unknown relative leaves me a big bundle..." or "when I win the lottery..." Clarence went to church one day and prayed that he would win the lottery. A week passed. No lottery win. He went again and prayed twice as long. A second uneventful week. He went the third time and pleaded, "Lord, just this once. Let me win. My job pays very little, and I have a wife and kids to feed." The Lord answered, "Just meet me halfway on this, Clarence. Buy a lottery ticket."

The ragged. In his first letter to the Corinthian community of believers, Paul began by reminding them that they "have been enriched in him, in speech, and knowledge of every kind"(1:5), but he has heard about divisions among them. Then he seemed to turn his attention to the troublemakers when he parenthetically discussed the subject of "wisdom"(1:18-2:16). His understanding of the broad stroke discipline of "wisdom" and those who are "wise" seems to be in contrast with the believers of Corinth who are not "wise by human standards." Not very many of them were powerful and of noble birth (1:26).

There is evidence, even from the accounts of the New Testament, that some upper-class folks became Christians. There was Dionysius (Acts 17), Sergius Paulus (Acts 13), high society ladies at Thessalonica and Berea (Acts 17), and the finance minister Erastus (Romans 16). Early Christian accounts identify the wife of the conqueror of Britain, Graecia, Flavius Clemens, the cousin of the emperor Domitian, and those of high rank alluded to by Pliny (see Barclay, *The Letters To The Corinthians*, Westminster: Philadelphia, 1975, p. 21).

"Nevertheless, the bulk of the membership probably did come from the lower economic and social classes. Not many would have had much education" according to Frederick Borsch. Christians of the first and second centuries, generally, were not well regarded by the rich and powerful. In fact, many of them were the sixty million slaves in the empire. A slave was a living tool, a piece of equipment, with no more rights than a donkey or a horse. Celsus, a Greek philosopher of the second half of the second century, noted, "we see them (the Christians) in their own houses, wool dressers, cobblers, and fullers, the most uneducated and vulgar persons…a swarm of bats—or ants creeping out of their nests…or frogs holding a symposium round a swamp—or worms in conventicle in a corner of mud" (Barclay, p. 21).

Paul wanted the uneducated and unpowerful believers of Corinth not to be intimidated by lofty intellectuals or "better than thou" members of the community. "You are not wise, not powerful, and not royals. But cheer up! You are wealthier than you think!"

The rich. Wealth in the kingdom has nothing to do with money, the accumulation of things, or high status in the community. Even those looked down by proper society may enter the kingdom. Think about Noah the drunkard, Abraham the liar who passed off his wife as his sister, Jacob who stole the birthright from his brother, Moses who was a murderer who lived in exile, as well as King David who committed adultery and ordered that his lover's husband be killed. Mary was a peasant teenager. Joseph was a blue-collar worker. Matthew was a tax collector who worked for the Romans. Peter was a hot-headed troublemaker. Paul, himself, was a former religious fanatic out to kill the followers of Jesus.

Saint Augustine was the father of an illegitimate child. Saint Francis of Assisi was a wealthy playboy. Martin Luther was the son of a coal miner.

"Wisdom" (or intellectualism or high social standing) has nothing to do with one's connection to God. Wisdom does not connect us to God; it is the branch that is connected to the vine that connects us to God. God reaches out in love to the masses and those who feel the love and see the love are connected to the source of love, not through worldly wisdom but through another kind of wisdom called faith.

As a student at a small church college, I elected a course titled "introduction to philosophy." The instructor was an older professor who stumbled into class using crutches. He sat down at a desk and began to talk. That's all he did. He just talked. He talked about the nature of God and the ontological, cosmological, and teleological, plus more, proofs for the existence of God. I wrote down what he said as rapidly as I could. There was a general consensus on campus that he graded our test papers by tossing them down a stairwell. Those that reached the bottom got the A's. In my early years of preaching, I introduced a lot of Greek philosophy into my sermons. But as time went on, I appealed more and more to simple biblical testimony: "Christ is risen! Christ is risen indeed!"

Philosophical arguments for the existence and nature of God have their place. But Paul does not suggest to his "uneducated" readers that they embark upon the study of Greek philosophy. If one understands what love is, then one is in the kingdom like Flynn.

One day, the great fourteenth-century German mystic, John Tauler, met a beggar on the highway and, as was his custom, greeted him with the words, "God give you a good day, my friend!" But the beggar answered curtly, "I thank God I have never had a bad day." Well, then," said Tauler, "God give you a happy life." But the beggar retorted, "I've never been unhappy." "What do you mean?" asked Tauler. The beggar replied, "When it is fine, I thank God; and when it rains, I thank God.

When I have plenty, I thank God; and when I am hungry, I thank God. And since God's will *is* my will and since whatever pleases him pleases me, why should I be unhappy?" "Who are you anyway?" asked Tauler. "I am a king," came the reply. "You, a king?" laughed Tauler, "where's your kingdom?" "In my heart," whispered the man in rags, "in my heart."

I have met, either in books or in person, many teachers of high academic status: Bultman, Panenberg, Barth, Thielicke, Abraham Heschel, Bonhoeffer, Gustaf Aulen', Dorothee Sollee. I trusted their books and their devotion to their faith, not only because they expressed themselves so elegantly but because they were "in the kingdom in their hearts."

But one "of the kingdom" doesn't need to be "wise" or intellectually proficient and profound. Early in my ministry I served at a small country church in northwest Ohio. One of the farm families included a girl with down syndrome. Whenever I visited, she laughed and hugged me tightly. She loved everyone at church on Sunday and everyone loved her. She knew about Jesus, and she gushed with his unconditional love. I read somewhere that Augustine once said that the river of faith is shallow enough for a lamb and deep enough for a hippopotamus.

The faith can be expressed in the simplest act of kindness or in the tomes of Thomas Aquinas. Luther's faith is currently wrapped up in no less than 55 volumes. The biblical scholar Tischendorf was visiting Saint Catherine's monastery on Mount Sinai in 1844 when he noticed what turned out to be 129 leaves from an old manuscript in a basket ready for the fire. When he looked a little closer, he recognized that they were from an ancient manuscript of the Old Testament, the edition written about 70 AD known as the *septuagint*. The monks allowed him to take 43 pages. When he returned to his home, he examined them carefully and discovered that the manuscript was from the fourth century. Six years later he returned to Mount Sinai to get the rest of the pages that turned out to be a copy of the New Testament today known as the *codex sinaiticus*, one of Christianity's most valuable links to the early writings of the Christians.

What was trash turned out to be treasure. The rags by the fire were one of the greatest finds of the century. The simple minded, poor, lower-class believers of corinth were reminded by Paul that they themselves, in their speech and in their deeds, were treasured by God. Rags were really riches.

Amen.

Getting Spiritual

Michelangelo left his position, high on his back, painting the ceiling of the Sistine chapel, in order to replenish his paint pallet. While standing at floor level, at his paint table, he suddenly heard a voice from on high, "Michelangelo! Michelangelo!" "Yes, Lord, what is it?" asked the great artist. "Repaint and thin no more!" commanded the creator of the world. Likewise, the voice from on high or, perhaps the voice from within, commands us to change our direction in life.

While at Ephesus, Paul heard disturbing news about the community of believers in Corinth. Perhaps his letter was like a "voice from on high" calling the members of the gathered community to change direction. One might say that they were not exactly living the spiritual life to which God through Paul called them. They were bickering among themselves, taking each other to court, and grouping themselves into cliques. Paul called them to "repent and sin no more." They were to abandon the "spirit of the world" and open themselves up to receive "the spirit that is from God" (1 Corinthians 2:12).

Paul called us to leave the life of the mundane world behind. In the early 1980s, fans of Olivia Newton-John may have, perhaps too zealously, listened to her voice from her most successful recording of her career, "Physical." The single was the most successful song on the in the 1980s. The song ended her legacy as a clean-cut pop superstar and, in spite of the controversy surrounding it, she became a sexy, assertive persona. In spite of her initial reaction when she first saw the lyrics, that it was "too cheeky," she reached for the big bucks and two million copies sold in the US encouraged the hearers to "Let's Get Physical." Without encouragement from Newton-John, long before her Advent into show business, the Corinth lifestyle was a clarion call to "get physical."

The letter to the Corinthians reminds us today that there is a tendency in our culture to be satisfied to be "unspiritual" (v. 14) the shift from unspiritual, or "unnatural," or "physical," or "worldly," is not an easy transformation. David Brooks, a writer for the New York Times, commented on television that Americans do not necessarily vote for moral political candidates anymore. About half of American voters are more concerned about getting politicians into office that will do what the voters want. Morality is irrelevant.

Very few citizens of renaissance Europe had the luxury of picking their rulers but that doesn't mediate Luther's scathing attack on worldliness. A worldly person, in the reformer's opinion, was like a pig who lies in the sty or on the manure pile. There it rests, snores, and thinks only of the whereabouts of husks and bran. It knows nothing of death; it fears no hell; it is happy about no heaven; it hopes for no future life. Husks and bran are its kingdom of heaven. People who think no farther than how they may live here on earth are just like that (from his sermon of August 15, 1531, on Titus 2:13, *What Luther Says*, Vol. III, Concordia Publishing House: St. Louis, 1972, 4965).

Dramatic words. Paul's "concern" about the lack of spirituality in the lives of the Corinthians comes close to Luther's ire. No less candid than Luther, he appeals to them "not to associate with anyone…who is sexually immoral, greedy, or is an idolater, reviler, drunkard, or robber, and so on" (1 Corinthians 5:9). What, perhaps, is he implying? If the shoe fits…..?

I once heard about a wealthy lady who used up three hours every morning taking her bath, enjoying a deep massage, and fastidiously allowing herself to be dressed by her maidservant. She then entered her chauffeur-driven limousine and went forth to spend the rest of her day in company with other unmotivated, boring people. Let's give her some slack. At Christmas, she went to the bargain basement of her local department store and bought her maid a fresh house dress.

A man once went to visit the royal tombs in Vietnam. Inside the dark caverns, old women hobbled before him, going from one exhibit to the next and lighting candles so that the tombs could be seen. When the visitors left the dark caverns, the old women blew out the candles and waited in the darkness for the nest visitors. The elderly guides lived and ate and slept in the darkness of the tombs. There are many who live in spiritual darkness.

Paul invited us to enter the inspiring world of spiritual life. The doorway to spiritual life is the door to God's spirit. "Now we have received not the spirit of the world, but the spirit that is from God, so that we may understand the gifts bestowed on us by God" (v. 12). To live in the spirit (apart from the world) is to grasp the spirit of God. Often have I experienced a change of opinion after taking the effort to try to understand, listen, and grasp the spirit of a person who I initially did not like. And so it is with God. The occasional brush with God is not enough. It takes concentration, time, meditation, and prayer to enter into the mind of God. One discovers the mind of God at prayer or through struggle with a crisis of life and comes away with Paul's mind and the spirit of God. Human wisdom has its place, but Paul discovered when he addressed the learned men of Athens that simple language sans "lofty words of wisdom" travels further. "Plausible words of wisdom" may make an impact on some in the world, but simple words colored by "the demonstration of the spirit" make a greater impact.

William Sloane Coffin, chaplain of Yale University and senior minister of Riverside Church in New York City, compared Jesus to a magician who called members of the audience to approach the stage to take part in the act. Jesus calls us to take part in the act. He doesn't perform solo while we sit around in incense scented temples repeating mantras. Jesus shared the limelight with fishermen, with a tax collector, and women normally left at home tending their ovens. Paul called us to come forward from the sidelines and join him on the missionary road. That road may be the road to the door of a neighbor in need, the road to help out at the local food pantry, or the road to a coffee house to have an honest talk about God.

William Barclay wrote about a drunkard who claimed that he was "captured by Christ." His friends at the local tavern made fun of him. "Surely a sensible man like you cannot believe in the miracles that the Bible tells about. You cannot believe that this Jesus of yours turned water into wine." The new convert replied, "I do not know about the miracles in the Bible but in my own house I have seen him turn beer into furniture."

I once heard a story about Sam Rayburn, the speaker of the House of Representatives. Rayburn served in various political offices during the terms of eight presidents. He received word one day that the teenage daughter of a DC newsman had died. Early the following morning, the journalist answered the door to find Rayburn standing there. He said, "I just came by to see what I could do to help." The flustered, grieving father replied, "I don't think that there's anything you can do, Speaker. We're making all the arrangements." Rayburn asked, "Have you made your coffee yet?" The reporter had not yet taken the time to put the coffee on. Sam headed straight for the kitchen to brew the coffee. The newsman remembered that Rayburn had an appointment with the president that morning. Rayburn replied, "I already called him and told him I had a friend who was in trouble, and I couldn't come."

Paul wrote to the brothers and sisters of Corinth, "I fed you with milk, not solid food, for you were not ready for solid food. Even now you are still not ready, for you are still of the flesh" (1 Corinthians 3:2). It takes a willingness and effort to grow in the faith. The brothers and sisters in Corinth had some looking to do before they started leaping. All of us have to keep our souls and hearts open for the continual coming of the spirit.

One of my religion teachers in college once invited his students to attend an evening talk in a college lounge. He explained that many people do not grow beyond their "Sunday school" understanding of religion. Thanks be to God, there are the faithful members of congregations who take on the responsibility to teach Sunday school. Rightly, the best way to teach young children is simply to tell Bible stories. (Leave out the "critical" interpretation. Let the stories stand on their own two legs.) The interpretive digging into the narrative should start with more mature, open minds. One of the big issues in my younger days were the troubling arguments centering on the creation accounts of Genesis. It is my opinion that the scientific theories about the Genesis of the universe are not in conflict with the biblical points about the ultimate source and reasons for the world. There are two different languages, each coming to the point from different angles, answering different questions, some scientific, some theological. But that's just me. Let the reader understand. Coming to a mature faith takes an open mind and patience. The folks at Corinth were at a beginning point. We don't know where they ended up, but we do know that charity is better than hoarding; tolerance is better than closed minds; reconciliation is better than fence building and estrangement.

Paul invited his readers to move on. If necessary, repent, listen to one another, agree to disagree, and sin no more, that is, live on with charity toward each other, patience, and prayerful openness to the coming of that spirit which would allow them to do two things: forge onward in the world and, at the same time, look toward the light of participation in God's spirit, the spirit which has come through and after Christ, the spirit that knocks at our hearts even now.

Amen.

Jesus At The Altar

Once a priest and a lawyer happened to end up together in line at the pearly gates The priest reached the check-in point first. Saint Peter, on duty that day, quickly pulled up the priest's file and noted that the clergyman had done a decent job performing his sacerdotal duties and, accordingly, could proceed to his fine slightly-used, one bedroom condo, all cleaned and ready for his occupancy. The priest lingered for a few moments and overheard the apostle's conversation with the next fellow in line, a lawyer. Saint Peter complimented the lawyer for his earthly achievements, welcomed him to the land of heaven, and gave him the key to his accommodations, described as a spacious and luxurious mansion. The priest approached the apostle and humbly inquired, "Why did the lawyer receive such luxurious quarters and, I, a priest, such humble accommodations?" "Oh," retorted Peter, "we get lots of priests up here but he's the first lawyer."

Frequently, in his letter, the writer to the Hebrews identified Jesus as a priest "after the order of Melchizedek." (see chapters 5, 6, and 7) no one knows who the author was but it seems that he was a Jew who knew Jewish scripture backward and forward. He seemed to be a scholar writing to Jewish scholars, perhaps in Rome about 80 AD. Those to whom he wrote were either converts to the faith of Jesus or were curious about the movement. The letter proclaimed that Jesus was exalted (not "resurrected"), called Jesus the "pioneer" of salvation, and identified Jesus as the perfect priest therefore chosen as the one who could "make a sacrifice of atonement for the sins of the people" (v. 17).

The writer to the Hebrews identified the baby who Mary presented at Jerusalem (Luke 2:22ff) as the future high priest who would someday make the perfect sacrifice (his own death) and, in the doing, defeat death and the devil, and declare that death is not to be feared. Jesus, although of divine origin, could accomplish his mission because he had become one hundred percent human (v. 17) a proper priest had to be human.

The letter therefore takes a potshot at anyone with docetist leanings who might have proclaimed a Jesus, born, died, and resurrected, to be really a faux human, a human who did not leave footprints in Palestinian sand. Early church teachers might have pointed to this letter as documentation close to the source that "(Jesus) was of the family of David, and of Mary, who was truly born, both ate and drank..." Ignatius, (died ca. 108 AD), and that "God became man, and it was the Lord himself who saved us." (Irenaeus) (died ca. 200).

Once a grandfather wanted to teach his grandson about US currency. He laid in a line a shiny penny, a nickel, a dime, a quarter, a fifty-cent piece, and a wrinkled dollar bill on the table and asked, "Now, Johnny, which of these pieces of money would you like?" Johnny picked the shiny penny and requested, "please wrap the penny in the dollar bill." The Nicene creed confesses that Jesus "was incarnate of the Holy Spirit and the Virgin Mary and became truly human." The penny wrapped in the wrinkled dollar bill says it all.

For reasons known only to our maker, Jesus needed to be fully human in order to bring about salvation.

That "salvation" is described as the act of destroying the devil, the "one who has the power of death," thereby alleviating our human fear of death. The gospel for this day, the presentation of our Lord, records the forewarning of Simeon delivered to Mary that Jesus would be "a sign that will be opposed"(Luke 2: 34) one could not have a worse adversary than the devil.

When the going gets rough, one can easily be tempted to enlist the aid of the devil. One Halloween night a traveler costumed as the devil ran out of gas in front of a country church where worshipers were joined in song and acclamation, celebrating their faith in Jesus. The "devil" entered the church to seek help. The worshipers scrambled in all directions, overturning chairs and heading to the exits. One poor lady was cornered by the "devil". Before the traveler unmasked himself, she pleaded, "I've been a member of this congregation for twenty years and I've been on your side all along!"

Heaven knows, we all need to conquer our fear of death. A popular professor of systematic theology was teaching in the classroom when one of his gifted candidates for an advanced degree was summoned and snatched by the Nazis to serve as a pilot in the Luftwaffe. Later, on the front lines of the Mediterranean, the young man shared in a letter to his beloved professor that he feared certain impending death. His mentor wrote to him, "...death is in fact an enemy, a contradiction.... does it not sever and destroy the bonds of life and friendship? Does it not take away the best of our youth and shatter the lives of thousands of others? Is it not really an unnatural disorder?"

The young man's mentor continued, "And now we know for certain that what dies in me is not an 'it' but an 'I,' an 'I' for which there is no substitute among all the comrades who march over my grave. In death I am really and irretrievably and in actual fact at my end. ... but at the same time, I am one whose history with God cannot stop, since I am called by my name and I am the friend of Jesus. The resurrected one is victorious and I stand within his sphere of power. ... it is his 'alien' life with which I am in fellowship and which brings me through everything and receives me on the other side of the gloomy grave"(Helmut Thielicke, *Death And Life*, Philadelphia: Fortress Press, 1970, pp. xxi-xxvi).

I once heard a story from Britain about a local parish vicar who was called to the bedside of an ailing bedridden parishioner. The elderly man wanted the vicar to teach him how to pray. The minister pointed to the empty chair pulled up to the side of the bed and said, "John, just imagine that Jesus is sitting on that chair and tell him your troubles." A few days later, John's daughter came to the parsonage to tell the vicar that she found her father in bed that morning sleeping blissfully his eternal sleep. His hand was stretched out and resting on the chair.

Fred Schiotz, the first president of the newly formed American Lutheran church in 1962, once told the story about a member of his congregation that had been shunned by the members of the congregation for an indiscretion. Pastor Schiotz, newly arrived as the pastor, was told that an old man was on his deathbed. The pastor went to the house and offered to read from the scriptures. The old man sat up straight in the bed and ordered the young cleric to leave the room. The pastor returned the next day and offered the bread and wine of communion. The stricken man knocked the bread and cup of wine out of the hand that held it. The young cleric would not give up. He returned the third day with his wife in tow and asked her to stand at the foot of the bed and sing an old Norwegian hymn. The weak patient looked intently at the soloist and tears began to flow from his eyes. The high priest of Hebrews had broken through the denial of a hard heart and offered the courage it took to deny the power of death and begin the process of stepping into the next world.

The writer to the Hebrews attempted to explain the mystery of Christ. In fact, no one can describe Christ in any human language. Those who attended the four ecumenical councils gave it their best shot. The creeds are organized into three sections: Father, Son, and Holy Spirit. The Trinity may seem like illogical nonsense to some but, at this moment in time, it's the best we can do. Any other attempts to describe God or even to name God have missed the mark. George Forell wrote in his textbook on the protestant faith that "it should be added that ultimately the person of Christ is … a secret of God's grace. No theological statement can exhaustively describe what is essentially an experience of the Christian individual within the Christian community" (*The Protestant Faith*, p. 179)

The writer of the Hebrews was a Hebrew writing to Hebrews. He spoke the language of those who would read what he had to say. Our task is to attempt also to speak about Jesus in a language that is dictated by the culture in which we live. Maybe the "high priest" angle won't do the job. Another young soldier about to perish on the Russian front wrote to Thielicke, "I really want to be clear about what may be relied upon to the end. Is it Christ?" (ibid, p. 88), the author of Hebrews might have responded to the young, scared soldier, "Yes, you can rely upon Christ all the way to the end." All of us who witness the terrible brutality of ruthless acts of violence of humans against human might also want to know, "can I rely upon Christ to the end?" Mary was also warned by Simeon on that day of presentation that "a sword will pierce your own soul too" (Luke 2:35). We all live in fear of the sword that will pierce our soul. The Hebrews writer says, "Do not fear that sword. Jesus, the high priest, will deal with the sword; you just live your life in the certainty that the door to the future has been opened to you by our friend."

Amen.

Bearers of Light

I once heard a story about my forebears, Pennysylvania Dutch Lutherans, who migrated from Eastern Pennsylvania over the Alleghenies to southern Ohio around 1800 AD. When they decided to replace the log church with a brick structure, the church council met at my grandpa Keener's farm. While cousin Mary was getting the lemonade ready in the kitchen, Grandpa, president of the council, suggested that a chandelier be installed in the church. Cousin John Seim spoke up, "I object. First of all, nobody knows how to spell it; secondly, no one knows how the play it, and, thirdly, what the new church will really need is more light."

The writer of 2 Peter wanted to shed some light on two concerns: declining faith in the second coming and false prophecy. Just to be transparent, it should be noted that most scholars do not think that the Apostle Peter wrote the letter. The language and context was different from 1 Peter (perhaps actually written by Peter) and, reading between the lines, it sounds like something that could have been written as late as the middle of the second century. Also, an examination of the lists of the New Testament canon revealed that the letter was added reluctantly late or lastly to the canon. Not a big deal. It was common practice in those days to speak in the voice of a well-known person (without the tools of IA) in order to communicate what that person would have said about a selected subject. We can acknowledge that even though the writer "used" the name and tradition of Peter the apostle, the letter sheds light on some issues in the church in the second century.

The writer of 2 Peter wanted folks to remember the event of the transfiguration. Why? What, in the community of believers in the second century, would be so important about the transfiguration recorded in Matthew, Mark, and Luke? A reading of the text reveals that, for the writer of 2 Peter, the memory of the transfiguration was a sign given on the mountain that Jesus would come again at the end of time to wrap up human history. Contrary to popular academic opinion, the transfiguration did not prefigure the resurrection of Jesus but, on the contrary, according to 2 Peter, it was a signpost to the second coming.

The Transfiguration was a "window" to the future. Once a businessman went to Atlantic City to see a client. He took advantage of the trip to check into a new hotel with spectacular views of the Atlantic Ocean. He promised a friend back home to describe the view from his room. The hotel guest wrote, "I have a sweeping view of the ocean from my window. The window is twelve feet, two inches long and four feet, eight inches high. It is divided into three panels. A scraping of the glass has disclosed its chemical formula. The steel frames are black and I am including an analysis of the chemical composition of the putty used to keep the glass in the frames. I am also sending the results of my analysis of the window-cleaning detergent used to cope with the salt spray. I hope you have enjoyed my study of the ocean."

The readers of 2 Peter had to be reminded that their view of the future was limited and fading. They had to look beyond even the resurrection, beyond that window, to see into the future. Remember the Transfiguration! Do not be shortsighted! See the window of the Transfiguration and look through it to the second coming of Christ!

To be complete, the Christian vision has to include the experience of the Transfiguration and its visionary promise of the new world. In 1989, I led a tour group to the Soviet Union. Our guide took the group to Red Square one day to stand in line for the viewing of Lenin's tomb. I was not excited about the venture. Why would anyone want to stand in a slow-moving line to view the remains of a dead man? But the line moved quickly past the armed soldiers into a bluish corridor leading down and around the center to the bowels of the monument. The mood of the procession turned quiet and reverent. We were entering hallowed ground. Finally, we entered the room in the center of the pyramid dominated by the beautiful glass case enshrining the corpus. Lenin appeared to have just fallen asleep. His physical presence, though waxy, the lighting in the room, the reverence of those who passed by, made an impression of sacredness upon me. I exited the enclosure into the light of day and was guided down a garden way framed by pictures of great Soviet leaders. That evening the members of my group discussed our experience over caviar and vodka that most of us did not touch. We agreed that we had experienced a carefully contrived religious experience. Lenin was a savior whose spirit permeated Soviet culture, politics, and vision of the future. If the writer of 2 Peter were with us today, certainly he would renounce promises of an earthly paradise established through human effort. The new heaven and earth he envisioned would have divine origins. His frustration stems from the denial by his peers of a future "last times" heralded by the second coming of Christ. The proper "full" gospel was neglected.

Therefore, his second concern was about interpreters of "scripture" who were not delivering the full load. The writer was pointing to Jewish scripture, especially the prophecies of the coming Messiah. And he was also referencing the gospels and works of Paul written in the first century obviously already being circulated (3:14f). At any rate, there were false "prophets" in the land who were causing confusion and ignorance. They were slanderers of angels (2:10), party animals (2:13), adulterers (2:14), waterless springs and mists driven by a storm (2:17), slaves of corruption (2:19), and scoffers indulging their own lusts (3:3). Their fate is nothing less than deepest darkness (2:17).

Why "deepest darkness" for those "who slander what they do not understand?" (2:12). Simply because they omit or bastardize "the words spoken in the past by the holy prophets, and the commandment of the Lord and Savior spoken through (the) apostles" (3:2). We don't know exactly what terrible blasphemous manure they were spreading around except that they were not preaching about "new heavens and a new earth" (3:13).

For 2 Peter, a gospel sans a vision of a new heaven and new earth was not the complete gospel. In fact, the gospel about Jesus Christ. Was not the gospel at all unless it was delivered in the wrappings of the promise of the coming of the day of the Lord.

Here would be the word to us today: Preach Christ crucified, resurrected, *and coming again!* Looking at the problem widely, we might conclude that present day "prophets" and "prophecies" and "teachings" should be evaluated against the historic teachings of the church. From the get-go, legitimate teachers must be those who walked and talked with Jesus and witnessed his resurrection. When the vacancy occurred on the council of the twelve disciples, Matthias was elected to fill the seat vacated by Judas because Matthias accompanied the disciples "from the baptism of John until the day when (Jesus) was taken up from us" (Acts 1:22). The writer of 2 Peter is a true teacher because he (placing himself into the persona and authority of Peter) had been an eyewitness of Jesus' majesty (1:16). Make no bones about it, the author of the letter maintained that his authority came from the great apostle Peter himself, with whose voice he spoke.

Today, most "preachers" willingly submit themselves to the authority of scripture as it stands and as it has been interpreted by conscientious theologians through the ages. I, for example, have been guided by my understanding of the scriptures gleaned by reputable interpreters like Augustine, Luther, Wesley, Calvin, Karl Barth, and male and female teachers at major divinity schools. I am also guided by the confessions of my church. Moreover, I am subject to the oversight of the teachers and leaders of my denomination. Those who subscribe to the confessions and more universal understanding of the scriptures stood aghast when a Jim Jones or Victor Paul Wierwille (The Way International) claimed to have greater authority than Jesus.

It seems to me that, through the power, inspiration, and presence of the Spirit, one can know who the legitimate teachers are and who are not. Take the doctrine of the Trinity, for example. That doctrine is (almost) universally understood as a hedge against false teaching because it lays out the scriptural view of the person and mission of Jesus. Jesus is God cast in human language and the one who empowers and guides the church today.

But the non-theologian is also guided by the Spirit. I knew a woman in the first parish I served in the soybean fields of northwest Ohio. She was burdened with much in her life. She had to live with the uncertainty of farm income from year to year. She had to care completely for a sister who had suffered a devastating stroke. She had to pick up pieces of hope and fortitude when her son, her only child, severely permanently injured himself in a motorcycle accident. Soon thereafter, her husband died from suddenly detected leukemia. Through the years, I kept in contact with her and watched her struggle with her own illness. Through it all, she relentlessly visited homebound people, took food to the hungry, sent donations to charitable causes, donated her time helping others to recover from tornado damage, and gave a parcel of her land to help a young newly married couple get a start in life.

Now who is the teacher? Who is the legitimate prophet? Who is the witness to the vision of that day of righteousness to come? They are those who are lamps "shining in a dark place" and who already possess "the morning star" (1:20). It is true. The gospel of Christ is not the complete package unless it imbodies the hope of that which is to come. We cross the line from this world into the next and see the perfection, the reconciliation, the perfect peace which is to come. Because that which is to come "where righteousness is at home" (3:13) is harbored in our hearts, we, as disciples of Christ, bring it to light in the midst of the vicissitudes of earthly existence. We are the chandeliers, casting the darkness and shadows of hopelessness back to the dark land whence they come.

Amen.